MESSAGE

OF

THE PRESIDENT OF THE UNITED STATES,

IN COMPLIANCE WITH

A RESOLUTION OF THE SENATE OF THE 11TH INSTANT, CALLING FOR INFOR-
MATION RESPECTING THE PROCEEDINGS OF THE REPRESENTATIVES
OF THE EUROPEAN POWERS, AT A CONGRESS HELD AT
PARIS, RELATIVE TO NEUTRAL RIGHTS.

AUGUST 13, 1856.—Read, and ordered to be printed; and ordered that 5,000 additional copies
be printed, 500 of which to be for the use of the State Department.

To the Senate of the United States:

I transmit a report from the Secretary of State, with accompanying papers, in answer to the resolution of the Senate of yesterday.

FRANKLIN PIERCE.

WASHINGTON, *August* 12, 1856.

DEPARTMENT OF STATE,
Washington, August 11, 1856.

The Secretary of State, to whom has been referred a resolution of the Senate of this date, requesting the President "to inform the Senate, if it be not in his opinion inconsistent with the public inter-est, whether the European powers which were represented at the late congress of plenipotentiaries assembled at Paris, or any of them, have communicated to this government the proceedings of that body in relation to neutral rights, with a view to obtain its concurrence therein; and what measures, if any, have been taken on the part of the United States upon that subject," has the honor to lay before the President the accompanying papers.

    Respectfully submitted.

W. L. MARCY.

To the PRESIDENT OF THE UNITED STATES.

[Translation.]

Extract from a despatch of his excellency Count Walewski to Count de Sartiges, May, 1856.

The plenipotentiaries assembled in the congress of Paris have come to an agreement on the terms of a declaration intended to settle the principles of maritime law in so much as it concerns neutrals during war. Herewith I have the honor to transmit to you a copy of that act, which fully meets the tendancies of our epoch, and at once puts an end to the useless calamities which a custom equally reprobated by reason and by humanity, superadded to those which fatally result from a state of war.

The congress have not overlooked the fact that their work, in order that it may prove complete, must secure the assent of all the maritime powers; since such governments only as shall have acceded to the arrangement can be mutually bound by it. On this score, we attach peculiar value to the concurrence of the United States, that will not consent, we confidently trust, to hold off from a concert of action which defines a new and essential progress in international relations.

The determination of the congress at Paris defines the object which it is intended to attain. The clashing constructions given to the rights of neutrals have, up to the last war, proved a source of deplorable conflicts; whilst privateering inflicted on the commerce and naviga-

MAY 3 1915

tion of non-belligerent states an injury so much the more grievous as it gave room for the most calamitous excesses.

These, count, are the events which, for our part, we are happy in striving to repel, and we feel convinced that the concurrence of the United States will not be withheld in a question every way worthy of the philanthropic spirit of the American people; a question which at once, and in a high degree, concerns the development and security of commercial transactions.

The plenipotentiaries sent to the congress have, as you may see in protocol No. 24, bound themselves, in the name of their respective governments, to enter, for the future, into no arrangement on the application of maritime law in time of war, without stipulating for a strict observance of the four points resolved by the declaration. The concurrence which we solicit at the hands of those governments which were not represented in the Paris conferences can, consequently, apply to those principles only laid down in said declaration, and which are indivisible.

LEGATION OF FRANCE IN THE UNITED STATES.

[Translation.]

Annex to Protocol No. 23.

DECLARATION.

The plenipotentiaries who signed the treaty of Paris, of the thirtieth of March, one thousand eight hundred and fifty-six, assembled in conference, considering—

That maritime law, in time of war, has long been the subject of deplorable disputes;

That the uncertainty of the law, and of the duties in such a matter, gives rise to differences of opinion between neutrals and belligerents, which may occasion serious difficulties, and even conflicts;

That it is, consequently, advantageous to establish a uniform doctrine on so important a point;

That the plenipotentaries assembled in congress at Paris cannot better respond to the intentions by which their governments are animated, than by seeking to introduce into international relations fixed principles in this respect;

The above mentioned plenipotentiaries, being duly authorized, resolved to concert among themselves as to the means of attaining this object ; and, having come to an agreement, have adopted the following solemn declaration:

1. Privateering is, and remains, abolished;

2. The neutral flag covers enemy's goods, with the exception of contraband of war;

3. Neutral goods, with the exception of contraband of war, are not liable to capture under enemy's flag;

4. Blockades, in order to be binding, must be effective ; that is to say, maintained by a force sufficient really to prevent access to the coast of the enemy.

The governments of the undersigned plenipotentaries engage to bring the present declaration to the knowledge of the States which have not taken part in the congress of Paris, and to invite them to accede to it.

Convinced that the maxims which they now proclaim cannot but be received with gratitude by the whole world, the undersigned plenipotentiaries doubt not that the efforts of their governments to obtain the general adoption thereof will be crowned with full success.

The present declaration is not and shall not be binding, except between those powers who have acceded, or shall accede, to it.

Done at Paris, the sixteenth of April, one thousand eight hundred and fifty-six.

[The signatures follow.]

[Translation.]

Protocol No. 24.—Sitting of April 16, 1856.

EXTRACT.

On the proposition of Count Walewski, and recognising that it is for the general interest to maintain the indivisibility of the four principles mentioned in the declaration signed this day, the plenipotentiaries agree that the powers which shall have signed it, or which shall have acceded to it, cannot hereafter enter into any arrangement in regard to the application of the right of neutrals in time of war, which does not at the same time rest on the four principles which are the object of the said declaration.

Mr. Marcy to Mr. Seibels.

DEPARTMENT OF STATE,
Washington, July 14, 1856.

SIR: The diplomatic representatives of several of the European powers, which were parties to the late Paris conference, have very recently presented to this government "the declaration relative to neutral rights" adopted at that conference, and, on behalf of their governments, asked the adhesion of the United States to it. It is presumed that the same course has been adopted by the confederated powers towards other nations. The United States have learned, with sincere regret, that, in one or two instances, the four propositions, with all the conditions annexed, have been promptly, and this government cannot but think unadvisedly, accepted without restriction or qualification.

It is well known that the United States, about two years since, opened negotiations with maritime nations for the general adoption of the second and third propositions contained in the Paris declaration, and that the fourth is but the annunciation of a principle of international law now universally recognised. The conditions which are to accompany the acceptance of the propositions of the Paris conference will, as a necessary consequence, defeat the negotiations of the United States for the adoption of the second and third of the series with every power which has adhered, or may determine to adhere, to " the declaration." In the first place, all the four propositions must be taken, or none ; and second, they must be taken not only indivisibly, but with the surrender of an important attribute of sovereignty— that of negotiating with any nation on the subject of neutral rights, unless such negotiations embrace all the propositions contained in the Paris " declaration." Any nation might well hesitate before making such a surrender.

Some of the powers which are parties to that "declaration," and many which are invited to concur in it, are under solemn treaty stipulations with the United States, and it is presumed they are with other nations, in which the right to resort to privateers is not only recognised, but the manner of employing them is regulated with great particularity. How the proposed new engagement can be reconciled with the faithful observance of existing treaty stipulations on the subject cannot be easily perceived.

I shall not, in this despatch, remark upon the incompatibility of these obligations, nor shall I now exhibit the views which this government entertains of the fatal consequences likely to result from the new doctrine now attempted to be introduced into the maritime code to most commercial nations, and especially to those which are not burdened, or may not choose to burden themselves, with large naval establishments.

The right of a commercial State, when unhappily involved in war, to employ its mercantile marine for defence and aggression, has heretofore proved to be an essential aid in checking the domination of a belligerent possessed of a powerful navy. By the surrender of that uncontested right, one legitimate mode of defence is parted with for a like surrender only in form by a strong naval power; but in effect the mutual surrender places the weaker nation more completely at the mercy of the stronger. While the former loses, the later gains by the mutual surrender, and the freedom of the seas is much more completely given up to a few great powers which have the means and disposition to maintain large navies. This government will more fully develop its views as to the operation of the first principle of the Paris "declaration,"—that in relation to the abandonment of the right to issue letters of marque,—in its reply to those powers which have invited its concurrence in that "declaration." The measure, unless it gives a full application to the principle upon which it is based, and is made to withdraw private property upon the ocean from seizure by public armed vessels, as well as by privateers, will be exceedingly injurious to the commerce of all nations which do not occupy the first rank among naval powers.

I am directed by the President to instruct you to present this general view of the subject to the government to which you are accredited, in the hope that it may be induced to hesitate in acceding to a proposition which is here conceived to be fraught with injurious consequences to all but those powers which already have, or are willing to furnish themselves with, powerful navies.

I am, sir, your obedient servant,

W. L. MARCY.

J. J. SEIBELS, Esq., &c., &c, &c., *Brussels.*

The same to the Ministers of the United States at Naples, Madrid, Stockholm, Copenhagen, Lisbon, Mexico, Nicaragua, Bogota, Caraccas, Rio de Janeiro, Buenos Ayres, Santiago de Chile, Lima, Quito, La Paz, and Hawaii.

Mr. Marcy to the Count de Sartiges.

DEPARTMENT OF STATE,
Washington, July 28, 1856.

The undersigned, Secretary of State of the United States, has laid before the President "The Declaration concerning maritime law," adopted by the plenipotentiaries of Great Britain, Austria, France, Prussia, Russia, Sardinia, and Turkey, at Paris, on the 16th of April, 1856, which the Count de Sartiges, envoy extraordinary and minister plenipotentiary of France, has presented in behalf of the emperor of the French to the government of the United States, for the purpose of obtaining its adhesion to the principles therein contained.

Nearly two years since, the President submitted, not only to the powers represented in the late congress at Paris, but to all other maritime nations, the second and third propositions contained in that "declaration," and asked their assent to them as permanent principles of international law. The propositions thus submitted by the President were :

"1. That free ships make free goods—that is to say, that the effects or goods belonging to subjects or citizens of a power or state at war are free from capture or confiscation when found on board of neutral vessels, with the exception of articles contraband of war."

"2. That the property of neutrals on board an enemy's vessel is not subject to confiscation, unless the same be contraband of war."

It will be perceived that these propositions are substantially the same as the second and third in the "declaration" of the congress at Paris.

Four of the governments with which negotiations were opened on the subject by the United States have signified their acceptance of the foregoing propositions   Others were inclined to defer acting on them until the return of peace should furnish a more auspicious time for considering such international questions.   The proceeding of the congress of the plenipotentiaries at Paris will, as a necessary consequence, defeat the pending negotiations with the United States, if the two following propositions contained in protocol No. 24 are acceded to: first, that the four principles shall be indivisible; and, second, that the powers which have signed or may accede to the "declaration" shall not enter into any arrangement in regard to the application of the right of neutrals in time of war, which does not, at the same time, rest on the four principles which are the object of said "declaration."

As the indivisibility of the four principles and the limitation upon the sovereign attribute of negotiating with other powers are not a part of the "declaration," any nation is at liberty to reject either or both, and to act upon the "declaration" without restriction, acceding to it in whole or in part. In deliberating on this important subject, it behooves all powers to consider, and, if they think proper, to act upon this distinction. All the powers which may accede to that "declaration" and the subsequent restrictions contained in the 24th protocol, will assume an obligation which takes from them the liberty of assenting to the propositions submitted to them by the United States, unless they at the same time surrender a principle of maritime law which has never been contested—the right to employ privateers in time of war.

The second and third principles set forth in the "declaration," being those submitted to other maritime powers for adoption, by this government, it is most anxious to see incorporated, by general consent, into the code of maritime law, and thus placed beyond future controversy or question. Such a result, securing so many advantages to the commerce of neutral nations, might have been reasonbly expected but for the proceedings of the congress at Paris, which require them to be purchased by a too costly sacrifice—the surrender of a right which may well be considered as essential to the freedom of the seas.

The fourth principle contained in the "declaration," namely: "Blockades, in order to be binding, must be effective; that is to say, maintained by a force sufficient really to prevent access to the coast of the enemy;" can hardly be regarded as one falling within that class with which it was the object of the congress to interfere ; for this rule has not, for a long time, been regarded as uncertain, or the cause of any "deplorable disputes." If there have been any disputes in regard to blockades, the uncertainty was about the facts, but not the law. Those nations which have resorted to what are appropriately denominated "paper blockades," have rarely, if ever, undertaken afterwards to justify their conduct upon principle ; but have generally admitted the illegality of the practice, and indemnified the injured parties. What is to be adjudged "a force sufficient really to prevent access to a coast of the enemy," has often been a severely contested question ; and certainly the declaration, which merely reiterates a general undisputed maxim of maritime law, does nothing towards relieving the subject of blockade from that embarrassment. What force is requisite to constitute an effective blockade, remains as unsettled and as questionable as it was before the congress at Paris adopted the "declaration."

In regard to the right to employ privateers, which is declared to be abolished by the first principle put forth in the "declaration," there was, if possible, less uncertainty. The right to resort to privateers is as clear as the right to use public armed ships, and as incontestable as any other right appertaining to belligerents. The policy of that law has been occasionally questioned, not, however, by the best authorities ; but the law itself has been universally admitted, and most nations have not hesitated to avail themselves of it; it is as well sustained by practice and public opinion as any other to be found in the maritime code.

There is scarcely any rule of international law which particular nations in their treaties have not occasionally suspended or modified in regard to its application to themselves. Two treaties, only, can be found in which the contracting parties have agreed to abstain from the employment of privateers in case of war between them. The first was a treaty between the King of Sweeden and the States General of the United Provinces, in 1675. Shortly after it was concluded the parties were involved in war, and the stipulation concerning privateers was entirely disregarded by both. The second was the treaty of 1785, between the United States and the King of Prussia. When this treaty was renewed, in 1799, the clause stipulating not to resort to privateering was omitted. For the last half century there has been no arrangement, by treaty or otherwise, to abolish the right, until the recent proceedings of the plenipotentiaries at Paris.

By taking the subject of privateering into consideration, that congress has gone beyond its professed object, which was, as it declared, to remove the uncertainty on points of maritime law, and thereby prevent "differences of opinion between neutrals and belligerents, and, consequently, serious difficulties and even conflicts." So far as the principle in regard to privateering is concerned, the proceedings of the congress are in the nature of an act of legislation, and seek to change a well settled principle of international law.

The interest of commerce is deeply concerned in the establishment of the two principles which the United States had submitted to all maritime powers, and it is much to be regretted that the powers represented in the congress at Paris, fully approving them, should have endangered their adoption by uniting them to another inadmissible principle, and making the failure of all the necessary consequence of the rejection of any one. To three of the four principles contained in the "declaration," there would not probably be a serious objection from any quarter, but to the other a vigorous resistance must have been anticipated.

The policy of the law which allows a resort to privateers has been questioned for reasons which do not command the assent of this government. Without entering into a full discussion on this point, the undersigned will confront the ordinary and chief objection to that policy, by authority which will be regarded with profound respect, particularly in France. In a commentary on the French ordonnance of 1681, Valin says:

"However lawful and time-honored this mode of warfare may be, it is, nevertheless, disapproved of by some pretended philosophers. According to their notions, such is not the way in which the state and the sovereign are to be served: whilst the profits which individuals may derive from the pursuit are illicit, or at least disgraceful. But this is the language of bad citizens, who, under the stately mask of a spurious wisdom, and of a craftily sensitive conscience, seek to mislead the judgment by a concealment of the secret motive which gives birth to their indifference for the welfare and advantage of the state. Such are as worthy of blame, as are those entitled to praise, who generously expose their property and their lives to the dangers of privateering."

In a work of much repute, published in France almost simultaneously with the proceedings of the congress at Paris, it is declared that—"The issuing of letters of marque, therefore, is a constantly customary belligerent act. Privateers are bona fide war vessels, manned by volunteers, to whom, by way of reward, the sovereign resigns such prizes as they make, in the same manner as he sometimes assigns to the land forces a portion of the war contributions levied on the conquered enemy."—(Pistoye et Duverdy, des Prises Maritimes.)

It is not denied that annoyances to neutral commerce, and even abuses, have occasionally resulted from the practice of privateering; such was the case formerly more than in recent times; but when it is a question of changing a law, the incidental evils are to be considered in connexion with its benefits and advantages. If these benefits and advantages can be obtained in any other way, without injury to other rights, these occasional abuses may then justify the change; however ancient or firmly established may be the law.

The reasons which induced the congress at Paris to declare privateering abolished are not stated, but they are presumed to be only such as are usually urged against the exercise of that belligerent right.

The prevalence of Christianity and the progress of civilization have greatly mitigated the severity of the ancient mode of prosecuting hostilities. War is now an affair of governments. "It is the public authority which makes and carries on war; individuals are not permitted to take part in it, unless authorized to do so by their government." It is a generally received rule of modern warfare, so far at least as operations upon land are concerned, that the persons and effects of non-combatants are to be respected. The wanton pillage or uncompensated appropriation of individual property by an army, even, in possession of an enemy's country, is against the usage of modern times. Such a mode of proceeding at this day would be condemned by the enlightened judgment of the world, unless warranted by special circumstances. Every consideration which upholds this sentiment in regard to the conduct of a war on land favors the application of the same rule to the persons and property of citizens of the belligerents found upon the ocean.

It is fair to presume that the strong desire to ameliorate the severe usages of war by exempting private property upon the ocean from hostile seizure, to the extent it is usually exempted on land, was the chief inducement which led to "the declaration," by the congress at Paris, that "privateering is, and remains, abolished."

The undersigned is directed by the President to say, that to this principle of exempting private property upon the ocean, as well as upon the land, applied without restriction, he yields a most ready and willing assent. The undersigned cannot better express the President's views upon the subject than by quoting the language of his annual message to Congress, of December 4, 1854:

"The proposition to enter into engagements to forego a resort to privateers, in case this couutry should be forced into a war with a great naval power, is not entitled to more favorable consideration than would be a proposition to agree not to accept the services of volunteers for operations on land. When the honor or rights of our country require it to assume a hostile attitude, it confidently relies upon the patriotism of its citizens, not ordinarily devoted to the military profession, to augment the army and navy, so as to make them fully adequate to the emergency which calls them into action. The proposal to surrender the right to employ privateers is professedly founded upon the principle that private property of unoffending non-combatants, though enemies, should be exempt from the ravages of war ; but the proposed surrender goes but little way in carrying out that principle, which equally requires that such private property should not be seized or molested by national ships of war. Should the leading powers of Europe concur in proposing, as a rule of international law, to exempt private property, upon the ocean, from seizure by public armed cruisers as well as by privateers, the United States will readily meet them on that broad ground.''

The reasons in favor of the doctrine that private property should be exempted from seizure in the operations of war are considered in this enlightened age so controlling as to have secured its partial adoption by all civilized nations; but it would be difficult to find any substantial reasons for the distinction now recognised in its application to such property on land, and not to that which is found upon the ocean.

If it be the object of the declaration adopted at Paris to abolish this distinction, and to give the same security from the ravages of war to the property of belligerent subjects on the ocean, as is now accorded to such property upon the land, the congress at Paris has fallen short of the proposed result, by not placing individual effects of belligerents beyond the reach of public armed ships as well as privateers. If such property is to remain exposed to seizure by ships belonging to the navy of the adverse party, it is extremely difficult to perceive why it should not, in like manner, be exposed to seizure by privateers, which are in fact but another branch of the public force of the nation commissioning them.

If the principle of capturing private property on the ocean and condemning it as prize of war be given up, that property would and of right ought to be as secure from molestation by public armed vessels as by privateers; but if that principle be adhered to, it would be worse than useless to attempt to confine the exercise of the right of capture to any particular description of the public force of the belligerents. There is no sound principle by which such a distinction can be sustained ; no capacity which could trace a definite line of separation proposed to be made ; and no proper tribunal to which a disputed question on that subject could be referred for adjustment. The pretence that the distinction may be supported upon the ground that ships not belonging permanently to a regular navy are more likely to disregard the rights of neutrals than those which do belong to such a navy, is not well sustained by modern experience. If it be urged

that a participation in the prizes is calculated to stimulate cupidity,
that, as a peculiar objection, is removed by the fact that the same pas-
sion is addressed by the distribution of prize-money among the officers
and crews of ships of a regular navy. Every nation which authorizes
privateers is as responsible for their conduct as it is for that of its
navy, and will, as a matter of prudence, take proper precaution and
security against abuses.

But if such a distinction were to be attempted, it would be very
difficult, if not impracticable, to define the particular class of the
public maritime force which should be regarded as privateers. "Deplorable disputes," more in number and more difficult of adjustment,
would arise from an attempt to discriminate between privateers and
public armed ships.

If such a discrimination were attempted, every nation would have
an undoubted right to declare what vessels should constitute its navy,
and what should be requisite to give them the character of public
armed ships. These are matters which could not be safely or pru-
dently left to the determination or supervision of any foreign power,
yet the decision of such controversies would naturally fall into the
hands of predominant naval powers, which would have the ability to
enforce their judgments. It cannot be offensive to urge weaker powers
to avoid as far as possible such an arbitrament, and to manintain with
firmness every existing barrier against encroachments from such a
quarter.

No nation which has a due sense of self-respect will allow any other,
belligerent or neutral, to determine the character of the force which
it may deem proper to use in prosecuting hostilities; nor will it act
wisely if it voluntarily surrenders the right to resort to any means,
sanctioned by international law, which, under any circumstances, may
be advantageously used for defence or aggression.

The United States consider powerful navies and large standing armies
as permanent establishments, to be detrimental to national prosperity and dangerous to civil liberty. The expense of keeping them
up is burdensome to the people ; they are, in the opinion of this government, in some degree a menace to peace among nations. A large
force, ever ready to be devoted to the purposes of war, is a temptation
to rush into it. The policy of the United States has ever been, and
never more than now, adverse to such establishments; and they can
never be brought to acquiesce in any change in international law
which may render it necessary for them to maintain a powerful navy

or large regular army in time of peace. If forced to vindicate their rights by arms, they are content, in the present aspect of international relations, to rely, in military operations on land, mainly upon volunteer troops, and for the protection of their commerce in no inconsiderable degree upon their mercantile marine. If this country were deprived of these resources, it would be obliged to change its policy and assume a military attitude before the world. In resisting an attempt to change the existing maritime law that may produce such a result, it looks beyond its own interest, and embraces in its view the interest of all such nations as are not likely to be dominant naval powers. Their situation in this respect is similar to that of the United States, and to them the protection of commerce and the maintenance of international relations of peace appeal as strongly as to this country, to withstand the proposed change in the settled law of nations. To such nations the surrender of the right to resort to privateers would be attended with consequences most adverse to their commercial prosperity without any compensating advantages. Most certainly no better reasons can be given for such a surrender, than for foregoing the right to receive the services of volunteers ; and the proposition to abandon the former is entitled, in the judgment of the President, to no more favor than a similar proposition in relation to the latter. This opinion of the importance of privateeers to the community of nations, excepting only those of great naval strength, is not only vindicated by history, but sustained by high authority. The following passage in the treatise on maritime prizes, to which I have before referred, deserves particular attention :

" Privateers are especially useful to those powers whose navy is inferior to that of their enemies. Belligerents, with powerful and extensive naval armaments, may cruise upon the seas with their national navies ; but should those States, whose naval forces are of less power and extent, be left to their own resources, they could not hold out in a maritime war ; whilst by the equipment of privateers they may succeed in inflicting upon the enemy an injury equivalent to that which they themselves sustain. Hence governments have frequently been known, by every possible appliance, to favor privateering armaments. It has even occurred that sovereigns, not merely satisfied with issuing letters of marque, have also taken, as it were, an interest in the armament. Thus did Louis the Fourteenth frequently lend out his ships, and sometimes reserve for himself a share navy the prizes.''

It certainly ought not to excite the least surprise that strong naval powers should be willing to forego the practice, comparatively useless to them, of employing privateers, upon condition that weaker powers agree to part with their most effective means of defending their maritime rights. It is, in the opinion of this government, to be seriously apprehended that if the use of privateers be abandoned, the dominion over the seas will be surrendered to those powers which adopt the policy and have the means of keeping up large navies. The one which has a decided naval superiority would be potentially the mistress of the ocean, and by the abolition of privateering, that domination would be more firmly secured. Such a power engaged in a war with a nation inferior in naval strength, would have nothing to do for the security and protection of its commerce but to look after the ships of the regular navy of its enemy. These might be held in check by one-half, or less, of its naval force, and the other might sweep the commerce of its enemy from the ocean. Nor would the injurious effects of a vast naval superiority to weaker States be much diminished if that superiority was shared among three or four great powers. It is unquestionably the interest of such weaker states to discountenance and resist a measure which fosters the growth of regular naval establishments.

In discussing the effect of the proposed measure—the abolition of privateering—a reference to the existing condition of nations is almost unavoidable. An instance will at once present itself in regard to two nations where the commerce of each is about equal, and about equally wide-spread over the world. As commercial powers they approach to an equality, but as naval powers there is great disparity between them. The regular navy of one vastly exceeds that of the other. In case of a war between them, only an inconsiderable part of the navy of the one would be required to prevent that of the other from being used for defence or aggression, while the remainder would be devoted to the unembarrassed employment of destroying the commerce of the weaker in naval strength. The fatal consequences of this great inequality of naval force between two such belligerents would be in part remedied by the use of privateers; in that case, while either might assail the commerce of the other in every sea, they would be obliged to distribute and employ their respective navies in the work of protection. This statement only illustrates what would be the case, with some modification, in every war where there may be considerable disparity in the naval strength of the belligerents.

History throws much light upon this question. France, at an early period, was without a navy, and in her wars with Great Britain and Spain, both then naval powers, she resorted with signal good effect to privateering, not only for protection, but successful aggression. She obtained many privateers from Holland, and by this force gained decided advantages on the ocean over her enemy. Whilst in that condition, France could hardly have been expected to originate or concur in a proposition to abolish privateering. The condition of many of the smaller States of the world is now, in relation to naval powers, not much unlike that of France in the middle of the sixteenth century. At a later period, during the reign of Louis the Fourteenth, several expeditions were fitted out by him, composed wholly of privateers, which were most effectively employed in prosecuting hostilities with naval powers.

Those who may have at any time a control on the ocean will be strongly tempted to regulate its use in a manner to subserve their own interests and ambitious projects. The ocean is the common property of all nations, and instead of yielding to a measure which will be likely to secure to a few—possibly to one—an ascendancy over it, each should pertinaciously retain all the means it possesses to defend the common heritage. A predominant power upon the ocean is more menacing to the well-being of others than such a power on land, and all are alike interested in resisting a measure calculated to facilitate the permanent establishment of such a domination, whether to be wielded by one power or shared among a few others.

The injuries likely to result from surrendering the dominion of the seas to one or a few nations which have powerful navies, arise mainly from the practice of subjecting private property on the ocean to seizure by belligerents. Justice and humanity demand that this practice should be abandoned, and that the rule in relation to such property on land should be extended to it when found upon the high seas.

The President, therefore, proposes to add to the first proposition in the "declaration" of the congress at Paris the following words: "And that the private property of the subjects or citizens of a belligerent on the high seas shall be exempted from seizure by public armed vessels of the other belligerent, except it be contraband." Thus amended, the government of the United States will adopt it, together with the other three principles contained in that "declaration."

I am directed to communicate the approval of the President to the second, third, and fourth propositions, independently of the first, should the amendment be unacceptable. The amendment is commended by so many powerful considerations, and the principle which calls for it has so long had the emphatic sanction of all enlightened nations in military operations on land, that the President is reluctant to believe it will meet with any serious opposition. Without the proposed modification of the first principle, he cannot convince himself that it would be wise or safe to change the existing law in regard to the right of privateering.

If the amendment should not be adopted, it will be proper for the United States to have some understanding in regard to the treatment of their privateers when they shall have occasion to visit the ports of those powers which are, or may become, parties to the declaration of the congress at Paris. The United States will, upon the ground of right and comity, claim for them the same consideration to which they are entitled, and which was extended to them, under the law of nations, before the attempted modification of it by that congress.

As connected with the subject herein discussed, it is not inappropriate to remark, that a due regard to the fair claims of neutrals would seem to require some modification, if not an abandonment, of the doctrine in relation to contraband trade. Nations which preserve the relations of peace should not be injuriously affected in their commercial intercourse by those which choose to involve themselves in war, provided the citizens of such peaceful nations do not compromise their character as neutrals by a direct interference with the military operations of the belligerents. The laws of siege and blockade, it is believed, afford all the remedies against neutrals that the parties to the war can justly claim. Those laws interdict all trade with the besieged or blockaded places. A further interference with the ordinary pursuits of neutrals, in nowise to blame for an existing state of hostilities, is contrary to the obvious dictates of justice. If this view of the subject could be adopted, and practically observed by all civilized nations, the right of search, which has been the source of so much annoyance and of so many injuries to neutral commerce, would be restricted to such cases only as justified a suspicion of an attempt to trade with places actually in a state of siege or blockade.

Humanity and justice demand that the calamities incident to war should be strictly limited to the belligerents themselves, and to those who voluntarily take part with them; but neutrals abstaining in good faith from such complicity ought to be left to pursue their ordinary trade with either belligerent, without restrictions in respect to the articles entering into it.

Though the United States do not propose to embarrass the other pending negotiations relative to the rights of neutrals, by pressing this change in the law of contraband, they will be ready to give it their sanction whenever there is a prospect of its favorable reception by other maritime powers.

The undersigned avails himself of this opportunity to renew to the Count de Sartiges the assurance of his high consideration.

W. L. MARCY.

The COUNT DE SARTIGES, &c., &c., &c.

The same to—

    Mr. EDWARD DE STOËCKL,
        Chargé d'Affaires of his Majesty the Emperor of Russia.

    BARON GEROLT,
        Envoy Extraordinary and Minister Plenipotentiary
                of his Majesty the Emperor of the French.

    The CHEVALIER HULSEMANN,
        Minister Resident of his Majesty the Emperor of Austria.

    The CHEVALIER BERTINATTI,
        Chargé d'Affaires of his Majesty the King of Sardinia.